LAST
/11 OX

4/10

R

DISASTER ALERT!

Preparing for disasters

Bobbie Kalman & Kelley MacAulay

Crabtree Publishing Company

www.crabtreebooks.com

Crabtree Publishing Company

www.crabtreebooks.com

Dedicated by Bobbie Kalman to Julia Largo and Priscilla Baker
I admire you both more than words can say. Thank you for being there when people need you the most.

Editor-in-Chief
Bobbie Kalman

Writing team
Bobbie Kalman
Kelley MacAulay

Photo research
Bobbie Kalman
Crystal Sikkens

Editors
Kathy Middleton
Julia Largo

Proofreader
Crystal Sikkens

Design
Bobbie Kalman
Katherine Berti

Production coordinator
Katherine Berti

Special thanks to
Consultants Julia Largo (Red Cross nurse volunteer)
and Priscilla Baker (Red Cross volunteer at many disasters)

Illustrations
Katherine Berti: page 26 (girl and bird silhouettes)

Photographs
American Red Cross: Daniel Cima: pages 24 (bottom left and right),
    28 (bottom right); Dennis Drenner: pages 5 (bottom), 21 (top); Talia
    Frenkel: cover (bottom left), pages 4, 14 (bottom), 20 (top)
BigStockPhoto: page 9 (windup radio and flashlight)
Marc Crabtree: page 11 (top)
FEMA: George Armstrong: cover (bottom right), page 31 (top); Jocelyn
    Augustino: page 28 (top); Bob Epstein: page 23 (top); Win Henderson:
    page 12 (top); Iowa Homeland Security and Emergency Management
    Division: page 17 (middle); Dave Saville: cover (top left), pages 11 (bottom),
    21 (middle)
Justin Hobson (An F5 tornado, June 22, 2007 in Elie, MB): page 16 (top)
Shutterstock: cover (top right), background (interior), pages 1, 3, 5 (top and
    middle), 6, 7, 8, 9 (all except windup radio and flashlight), 10, 11 (kittens),
    12 (middle and bottom), 13, 14 (top), 15, 16 (bottom), 17 (top and bottom),
    18 (top), 19, 20 (bottom), 21 (bottom), 22, 23 (bottom), 24 (top left), 25, 26
    (except girl and bird silhouettes), 27, 28 (bottom left), 29, 30, 31 (except top)
Other images by Photodisc and Weatherstock

Library and Archives Canada Cataloguing in Publication

Kalman, Bobbie, 1947-
    Preparing for disasters / Bobbie Kalman and Kelley MacAulay.

(Disaster alert!)
Includes index.
ISBN 978-0-7787-1589-4 (bound).--ISBN 978-0-7787-1621-1 (pbk.)

    1. Emergency management--Juvenile literature. I. MacAulay,
Kelley II. Title. III. Series: Disaster alert!

HV551.2.K34 2010   j363.34'7   C2009-903223-6

Library of Congress Cataloging-in-Publication Data

Kalman, Bobbie.
    Preparing for disasters / Bobbie Kalman and Kelley MacAulay.
        p. cm. -- (Disaster alert!)
    Includes index.
    ISBN 978-0-7787-1621-1 (pbk. : alk. paper) -- ISBN 978-0-7787-1589-4
(reinforced library binding : alk. paper)
    1. Emergency management--Juvenile literature. 2. Disasters--Juvenile
literature. I. MacAulay, Kelley. II. Title.

HV551.2.K35 2009
613.6'9--dc22

                                        2009021499

Crabtree Publishing Company

www.crabtreebooks.com   1-800-387-7650

Published in Canada
Crabtree Publishing
616 Welland Ave.
St. Catharines, Ontario
L2M 5V6

Published in the United States
Crabtree Publishing
PMB16A
350 Fifth Ave., Suite 3308
New York, NY 10118

Published in the United Kingdom
Crabtree Publishing
White Cross Mills
High Town, Lancaster
LA1 4XS

Published in Australia
Crabtree Publishing
386 Mt. Alexander Rd.
Ascot Vale (Melbourne)
VIC 3032

Table of Contents

What are disasters?

Disasters happen around the world every day. They often happen without warning. Disasters are events that change the lives of people in huge ways! Preparing for disasters can help lessen the shock. During disasters, people can lose their homes, possessions, families, friends, and pets. There are two main kinds of disasters—**natural disasters** and **human-made disasters**. Natural disasters are disasters that are caused by events in nature. Hurricanes, tornadoes, and earthquakes are natural disasters. Human-made disasters are disasters that are caused by the actions of people. This book provides information about disasters and how people can prepare for them.

Floods can happen anytime and anywhere. This boy is stranded on a flooded street.

Ready to respond

Most communities have teams of people who are ready to respond during and after disasters. These teams of **first-responders** include police officers, firefighters, paramedics, and doctors and nurses. First-responders work in the community every day, keeping people safe and healthy. Other helping teams are made up of volunteers who work for organizations such as the Red Cross and Salvation Army. These teams of volunteers are trained to prepare communities for disasters and to help people cope and rebuild their lives afterward.

Reduce the strain

Just after a disaster occurs, community helpers and volunteers are very busy. They may not be able to help all the people in a community immediately. People who are prepared for disasters, however, can help both themselves and others within their communities. Being prepared greatly reduces the burden on community helpers and volunteers.

These Red Cross volunteers are unloading supplies that were brought to a disaster area from another part of the country.

Firefighters fight fires of all kinds. These firefighters are putting out a house fire. A fire in the home is the most common type of disaster.

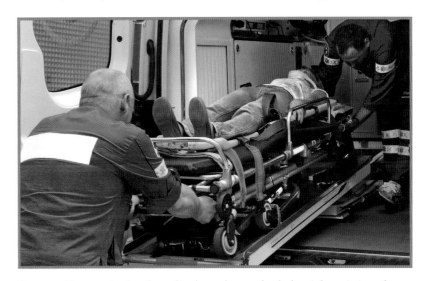

Paramedics are trained medical workers who help sick or injured people and get them to the hospital in ambulances.

Create a kit

Think about how many things you use every day—clothes, food, water, dishes, television sets, cars, lights, money, plus the many items you use to keep clean and stay healthy. During disasters, it is often very hard for people to gather together the items they need. To be prepared for a disaster, every family should have a **disaster-supply kit**. A disaster-supply kit is a collection of all the things a family might need during a disaster.

For home use

Disaster-supply kits can be used to **shelter-in-place**. To shelter-in-place is to protect yourself at home or wherever you are. People who live in areas where there are tornadoes can stock a **safe room** with supplies they may need, should a tornado hit their home. A safe room is a room that protects people from flying **debris**. It can be in a basement or elsewhere under the ground. Disaster kits can be taken to disaster shelters, as well. People who need to **evacuate**, or clear out, from an area by car can take a kit with them to have supplies on their journey to another town.

Many people who live in areas with frequent tornadoes have shelters outside their homes.

Many items in a family's disaster-supply kit should be kept in large, sturdy containers. The containers should have wheels, as they may be too heavy to carry when the supplies have been loaded into them. Large waterproof suitcases or plastic trash cans work well. Every member of the family must know where the disaster-supply kit is kept in the home.

Food supply

A disaster-supply kit that will be used to shelter-in-place should have at least a three-day supply of **non-perishable foods** for each member of the family. Non-perishable foods are foods that will not spoil, such as canned foods or foods in **Tetra Pak cartons**. Healthy foods to include are soups, beans, stews, milk powder or protein powder, dried fruit, whole-grain cereals, granola bars, and nut butter. Make sure your family likes the foods you pack. You also need to have plenty of water for drinking and washing.

Water and other essentials

Each person should have three gallons (11 liters) of water a day for at least three days. Make sure the water is stored in plastic containers that will not break. You can also pack fruit and vegetable juices to drink. Finally, you need to include utensils, dishes, a manual can opener, and a portable stove. Before using a stove, listen to the radio to make sure there is not a gas leak in your area. Using a stove or any other heat source when there is a gas leak could cause an explosion.

granola bars

canned foods

water

pot or pan for cooking

multi-purpose tool

Milk, juices, soups, and other foods come in Tetra Pak cartons, which are lighter than cans.

nut butter

plastic dishes

portable stove

Include at least a one-week supply of food for every pet in your home, as well as a half gallon (2 liters) of water per day for each pet.

Important supplies

You will need to pack clothing, **toiletries**, and some tools in your disaster kit. You will also need to communicate with others in your community. Cell phones and radios are important. Many people forget about money. They think their credit cards will get them through, but bank machines may not work during disasters. Ask your parents to make sure they always have, at home, some money in small bills, as well as some coins for telephone use. It is also a good idea to make copies of important papers, such as bank information, health insurance, and passports.

Clothing

Having the proper clothing during disasters not only helps keep people comfortable, but it also helps them stay healthy. Make sure you pack casual clothing, such as track suits, jeans, and sturdy, comfortable shoes for each member of the family. Packing extra underwear will help you feel clean when you cannot have a bath or shower.

What kind of weather?

Remember to consider the weather before choosing clothing for your kit. For example, if natural disasters such as blizzards often occur in your community, you should pack warm winter clothes, including hats and gloves in the kits. However, if natural disasters in your area occur more often in warm weather, the way tornadoes do, then pack light summer clothing. Also, make sure you try on the clothing in the kit every six months to make sure it all still fits!

winter coat

hat, scarf, and mittens

jeans

comfortable shoes

8

Other items

There are many other items you should include in your disaster-supply kit, such as:

- a first-aid kit stocked with antibiotic creams, bandages, latex gloves, medical tape, a first-aid manual, and prescription medications that people in your family take
- soap and other toiletries
- several packages of wet cleansing cloths (These may be your only way to wash yourself if there is no water!)
- a sleeping bag or blanket, sheet, pillow, and a towel for each family member
- any items needed for pets, such as collars with ID tags, leashes, cat litter, travel cages, food and water bowls, vaccination records, and a favorite blanket and toy
- windup or regular flashlights and extra batteries so that people can see in the dark in case of a **blackout**, or a loss of electricity
- matches in a waterproof container
- a tent large enough for the family
- a map of your city (see page 13)
- books, art supplies, music, playing cards, to help you feel calm and to pass the time
- a whistle to call for help (see page 25)
- extra car and house keys

cleansing cloths

first-aid kit

prescription medications

windup radio and flashlight

towels

sleeping bag

whistle

Ways to communicate

Make sure you include a windup or other portable radio and extra batteries in your kit. Before and after disasters, community helpers communicate with people by sending out instructions over the radio. For example, people may be instructed to stay in their homes if conditions outside are not safe. You should also include a cell phone in your kit. Phone lines are often damaged during disasters, leaving people unable to use the phones in their homes. People may be able to use cell phones to contact family members or community helpers, however. Don't forget to include a list of important telephone numbers, including those of family members.

9

Home evacuation

During some disasters, it may be necessary for people to evacuate, or leave, their homes. Every family should have a **home-evacuation plan** to put into action during disasters. A home-evacuation plan is a set of instructions that each member of the family uses to get safely out of the home and to a meeting place. Creating a plan ahead of time helps people feel calmer and more in control when disasters occur.

Multiple routes

To create a home-evacuation plan, gather together all the members of your family for a meeting. Discuss the possible routes you can use to get out of your home during a disaster. Your family must plan multiple escape routes, in case one of the routes is blocked during a disaster. By having more than one escape route planned, the members of your family will always have a way to get out of your home.

The meeting place

Next, your family must choose a meeting place outside the home. The meeting place is the location to which family members will go once they have escaped the house. A good meeting place is the front yard of the house across the street from your home.

You and your family must practice your evacuation plan at least every six months. Create quizzes to help your family review the routes out of the house, the name and number of the people to contact in an emergency, and the location of your meeting place.

Know where to take your pets!

Pets are not allowed in disaster shelters. People must make plans to get their pets safely to shelters that will care for animals during disasters. Veterinarians and volunteers at pet shelters care for the animals and return them to their owners after the disasters are over. People can contact their local humane societies to learn about disaster shelters for animals in their communities. Make sure your pets are wearing ID tags!

Animal shelters also take in animals that become lost or injured during a disaster. These people are rescuing dogs after a hurricane. The dogs will be taken to an animal shelter.

Community evacuation

Disasters can cause chaos and panic in communities, but people panic less when they know what to do. Many communities have evacuation plans to get people safely through a disaster. Community evacuation plans often include warning signals that alert people about dangers. Radio broadcasts then provide instructions on where people should go and how and when to get there.

Warning signals

Many communities have **sirens** placed around the town or city. Sirens are devices that send out loud warning signals before or during a disaster. These warning signals let people know that they need to go to a safe place and to turn on a radio or telelevision set. The local radio and television stations broadcast easy-to-understand instructions about what people should do. If there is enough warning about a disaster, people will be told to evacuate their community. If there is not enough time to leave the community, people will be instructed to go to disaster shelters (see pages 14-15.)

sirens

Following instructions

When people are instructed to evacuate their communities or go to disaster shelters, they will be advised about which streets to take. People must follow these instructions! Other streets in the community may be blocked by fallen trees or power lines. Every family should know ahead of time to which emergency disaster shelter they should go and how to get there. People who live in areas where natural disasters often occur should always have at least a half tank of gas in their cars so they can evacuate their city or drive to emergency shelters. Family members may need to use the maps in their disaster-supply kits to follow the directions given on the radio or television. Practice reading local maps ahead of time to become familiar with street names and learn which routes to follow.

Practice reading maps with your parents. Learn where you would go in a disaster.

Safe shelter

The buildings in your community may seem sturdy, but most may not be strong enough to stay standing in a natural disaster. Disaster shelters are built strong enough to withstand disasters, however. They give people safe places to stay during hurricanes or tornadoes.

Going to shelters

Many large communities have disaster shelters in each neighborhood. Most shelters are prepared before disasters occur. Volunteers stock the buildings with water and blankets. If people are instructed to evacuate to a shelter, they must do so immediately. People who leave from home should take as much of their disaster kits as they can carry with them to the shelters.

A Red Cross volunteer talks to a young girl at a disaster shelter.

Shelter-in-place

When disasters happen without warning, people may not have time to evacuate to disaster shelters. In these situations, they will be advised through radio and television broadcasts to shelter-in-place and protect themselves there.

Find a safe area

If your family is at home, lock all the doors and windows in your home. Next, gather everyone in an **interior room**. An interior room is one in the middle of the house, which has no walls facing the outside. Remember to bring your disaster-supply kit to this area!

When a tornado hit her town, this woman and her family moved into an underground shelter beside their home. She is happy to be alive!

If you are sheltering-at-home, lock all your doors and move into a basement room without windows. The room on the right is in the middle of the house and is under ground. It is the safest room.

Preparing for tornadoes

Tornadoes are the most violent storms on Earth. They are funnels of rotating wind that move at speeds of up to 300 mph (483 km/h). Tornadoes move unpredictably over the land. A tornado may rip apart one house and leave another home nearby completely untouched.

Learn the warning signs

There are many warning signs that tell people a tornado is about to occur. Before a tornado forms, the sky often becomes dark green in color. The clouds tower high in the sky, and large hail often falls. If a tornado is moving toward you, you will hear a very loud sound that is similar to the sound of a freight train. By learning the warning signs, people will have time to move to a safe place before the tornado reaches their area.

Each year, about 1,000 tornadoes occur in the United States. Over 300 of these tornadoes form in Tornado Alley. Tornado Alley is a wide area of land near the middle of the United States. Eighteen states, including Kansas, Texas, and Oklahoma, are part of Tornado Alley. Tornadoes also occur in other parts of North America, including many parts of Canada. The tornado in the top picture occurred in Manitoba, Canada.

Know where to go

If a tornado is on the way, go indoors immediately! The safest place to be is in a tornado shelter. If you cannot get to a disaster shelter, go to the basement or to the lowest floor of your house. Flatten yourself against an interior wall that does not face outdoors. You could also get into a closet on the lowest floor or under a piece of heavy furniture, such as a desk. Make sure you are not near any windows. Use your arms or a pillow to cover and protect your head.

Cover your head with a pillow or a thick blanket.

Last-ditch effort

If you are outside during a tornado and cannot get inside, lie face-down in a ditch and cover your head with your arms. If you are in a car, get out of it and run as far away from it as possible. The powerful winds of a tornado may get under the car and toss it through the air. You should also get out of a mobile home for the same reason.

Try to get to a tornado shelter, if you can.

After a tornado

- Call for help if any people in your family have been injured. Use the telephone only for emergency calls.
- Leave a building if you smell gas or chemical fumes.
- In case family members are separated from one another during a tornado, have a plan for getting back together. Ask an out-of-state relative or friend to serve as the "family contact." Make sure everyone in the family knows the phone number of the contact person.

Tornadoes can cause terrible damage to homes.

Huge hurricanes

Hurricanes are powerful storms with very strong winds. The winds swirl around a calm center called an **eye**. All hurricanes begin over warm ocean waters. When they roar onto coasts, these huge storms have enough force to destroy entire communities.

eye of hurricane

Surging onto land

A hurricane is a storm with winds that blow at least 74 mph (120 km/h). As a hurricane blows toward land, its fast-moving winds often push enormous amounts of water toward shore.

When the storm reaches land, the water becomes a **storm surge**, or huge wave of water. The wave rushes onto land, causing deep floods. The hurricane's winds topple trees and rip apart buildings. People may drown or get trapped in the buildings.

Preparing for the storm

People often have advance warning that a hurricane is headed toward their community. Whenever possible, they are evacuated from their community before the storm hits. Evacuation greatly reduces the number of lives lost. In some communities, however, people may not be able to leave. If you are staying at home, your family must prepare for the storm in these ways:

- Bring all outdoor objects, such as lawn furniture, bicycles, trash cans, and garden equipment, inside your home or garage to stop these items from being carried away by the wind and hurting people or damaging property.
- Nail boards over all the windows and glass doors in the home to prevent the glass from shattering in the wind. The boards should be measured and cut before the storm.
- Store extra water by filling clean bathtubs, sinks, and jugs.

Your family can prevent damage to your home by nailing wooden boards over the windows.

Fill sinks, bathtubs, and jugs with water.

storm surge

This photograph shows how a storm surge could topple buildings and cover city streets with water.

Flooding the land

Flooding is a common natural hazard. It can happen anywhere, at anytime. Hurricanes often cause huge floods. Storm surges can cover towns and cities in minutes! Flooding also happens during heavy rainfalls, when rivers overflow, when snow melts too fast, and when **dams** or **levees** break. Flooding may be only small amounts of water, or it may cover a house to the rooftop. Floods that happen very quickly are called **flash floods**.

Flood warnings

When the weather service issues a **Flood Watch**, it means flooding may happen soon. Stay tuned to the radio or television news for more information. A **Flood Warning** means that you may be asked to leave the area. A flood may be happening or will happen very soon. A **Flash-Flood Warning** means a flash flood is happening. If you hear a flood or flash-flood warning, talk to an adult immediately and get to high ground as soon as possible.

This girl's home and street are flooded. The only way she can get from one place to another is by boat.

These two photographs show how deep floods can be. Houses, roads, and cars are engulfed by water.

Preparing for floods

- Help your parents move as many belongings as possible to floors that are above ground level. Bring outdoor furniture indoors.
- Remove toxic substances such as pesticides and paints from low areas.
- Leave your home immediately and do not return until authorities tell you that it is safe to do so. If you must leave your home, remember to bring your disaster-supply kit, and to make arrangements for your pets.

To keep water out, many people place sandbags along the shores of rivers and in front of buildings.

Getting out

- Make sure your parents follow the evacuation routes and do not take shortcuts. They could lead you to blocked or dangerous areas.
- Avoid crossing bridges if the water is high and flowing quickly.
- Never cross a flooded area on foot or by car. The water may be deeper than it looks, and your car could get stuck or swept away.
- Make arrangements for pets.
- In your mailbox, leave a note with information about the time you left and where you went.

If possible, find a safe place for your pets. This dog is being rescued by a volunteer.

Animals will find higher ground during a flood. If you live on a farm, help your parents make sure that there are no obstacles in the way of your animals getting to a safe place on their own.

21

When the Earth shakes

During an earthquake, the ground shakes violently, sometimes causing huge buildings to crumble into piles of rubble. Earthquakes are caused deep inside the earth, along **plate boundaries**. Plate boundaries are areas where enormous rocks called **plates** slowly move past one another. Sometimes two plates grind together until they skid quickly past each other. As the plates shoot past each other, an earthquake occurs at the Earth's surface.

plate

plate

*Scientists use observation **satellites** and other tools to measure the movements of Earth's plates. A satellite is a human-made structure that circles Earth to gather information about it.*

*This picture shows a large **fault**, or break, within the Earth's **crust**, or top layer. Most earthquakes happen at faults.*

Preparing your home

If you live in an area along plate boundaries, your parents need to secure your home in certain ways. They can attach large appliances, such as refrigerators, to walls using metal straps. They should also move heavy objects that could fall off shelves. If there are beds beneath windows in your home, move them to safer areas. Hanging large mirrors should be avoided in earthquake-area homes. Glass can shatter and cause serious injuries.

Drop, cover, and hold on!

- If you are inside a building when an earthquake occurs, get under a desk or table. Heavy furniture can protect you from falling objects and breaking glass.
- Hold onto the legs of the furniture and be ready to move with it. If the shaking causes the furniture to move forward, crawl forward to stay under it. Stay in this position until the ground stops shaking.
- If there is no heavy furniture in the room, flatten your body against an interior wall in the building. Stay away from windows or any furniture that could fall over, such as a bookcase.
- If you are outdoors when an earthquake occurs, move quickly to an open area, where there are no buildings or structures that could collapse on top of you.
- If you are in a car, stay in the car and ask the driver to slow down and drive to a clear place. Ask him or her to avoid bridges or ramps that may have been damaged by the quake.
- Be cautious after an earthquake. Stay out of damaged buildings. Leave the area if you smell gas or fumes from chemicals. Open closet and cupboard doors carefully!

Earthquakes are common in areas where plate boundaries are, such as Alaska, California, British Columbia, Japan, and Taiwan. An earthquake in Northridge, California ripped apart this building.

Beware of more shocks!

Be prepared for **aftershocks**. Aftershocks are small earthquakes that cause more damage and can cause already-damaged structures to collapse. Aftershocks can occur hours, days, weeks, or even months after an earthquake.

Icy winter storms

In winter, **blizzards** and ice storms can hit suddenly, burying communities beneath layers of snow and ice. Blizzards are fierce winter storms with freezing temperatures. During a blizzard, winds often blow at 35 mph (56 km/h) or faster. These winds whip snow through the air, reducing visibility, and making driving very dangerous. Both blizzards and ice storms can cause blackouts. During blackouts, entire communities can lose power, often for many days.

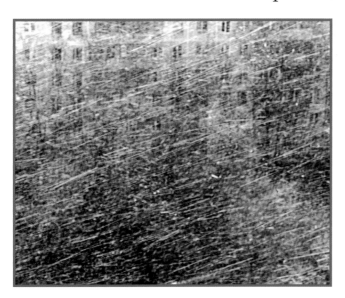

Ice all around

An ice storm is **freezing rain** that builds up at least one quarter inch (.635 cm) on surfaces. Freezing rain is rain that turns to ice when it hits the ground or another surface. Ice storms cover trees, buildings, roads, and sidewalks in thick layers of ice. This ice is very heavy and can cause huge tree limbs to snap off and crash to the ground. Roofs of buildings sometimes collapse under the weight of the ice.

Tree branches break off from the heavy weight of ice.

Blackouts during ice storms may take weeks to fix.

24

Winter-storm safety

If possible, stay indoors during blizzards and ice storms. If you have to go outdoors, dress in loose, warm layers of clothing. Wear heavy gloves, socks, and boots to reduce the risk of frostbite. Cover your mouth with a scarf to warm the air you breathe. If the power in your home goes out during a winter storm, turn off appliances and electronic equipment, such as computers and television sets, which were on when the power went out. Turning appliances off will prevent a second outage from occurring when power is restored.

reflective vest
warning triangle

snow brush

Car kits

People should always have at least a half tank of gas in their car in winter. Your family may need it to heat the car if you are stuck. A disaster-supply kit should be kept in every car for emergencies. Car disaster-supply kits could be lifesavers to people who are trapped in their cars during blizzards. Below are some important items that should be included in the kit:

- a shovel to dig snow from around your car
- brushes and ice scrapers to remove snow and ice from the car (A broom works well for cleaning off thick piles of snow.)
- blankets and towels
- paper towels, tissues, and wet cleansing cloths
- matches in a waterproof container and a candle in a tin container (The candle will provide heat and light inside the car.)
- flares, flashlights, and batteries
- a warning triangle and a reflective vest
- a cell phone
- a first-aid kit
- bottled water and granola bars
- a multifunctional tool
- a whistle (Three blows on a whistle or three flashes of a flashlight mean, "I need help.")

cell phone
first-aid kit
ice scraper
snow shovel
broom
whistle
flashlight

Pandemic!

People catch **viruses** every day. Viruses are illnesses that can spread easily from person to person. Many viruses, such as **influenza**, or the flu, can be treated by doctors. Sometimes, however, a new virus comes along, for which there is no treatment. Viruses can spread serious diseases through communities and, sometimes, around the world. In June 2009, the H1N1 flu was declared to be a **global pandemic** by the World Health Organization. A pandemic is an outbreak of a disease that has spread around the world.

virus

H1N1

The H1N1 flu started in Mexico and quickly spread to other parts of the world. Its symptoms are similar to the symptoms of the flu that people get during the winter months. Although the symptoms are not worse than those of the regular flu, healthcare workers fear that the virus may change and become more dangerous during the flu season.

During a pandemic, people often wear masks to filter germs out of the air they breathe.

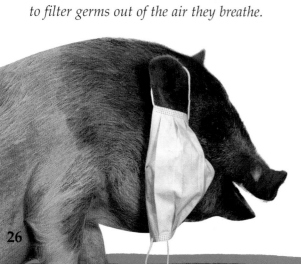

At first, the H1N1 flu was referred to as "swine flu," but this virus also contains genes similar to viruses found in birds and humans. Pigs can get H1N1 from humans, but people cannot get this virus by eating pork.

Stop the spreading!

Viruses spread easily. They usually spread when someone touches a person who has the virus and then touches his or her own face. Viruses also spread when people touch surfaces with infected liquids on them and then touch their faces. For example, when sick people cough or sneeze without covering their mouths, their saliva lands on surfaces such as tables. The saliva has the virus in it. When other people touch the table and then touch their faces, they can catch the virus. You can do these things to stop a virus from spreading:

- Cover your mouth when you cough or sneeze. Use a tissue or cough or sneeze into your sleeve. If you use a tissue, throw it away.

Wash your hands!

Wash your hands often. When you wash your hands, wet them under warm water and then add some soap and rub your hands together. Continue to rub them together while you count to twenty or sing the Happy Birthday song twice. Then rinse your hands under warm water. You should wash your hands each time:

- you come into contact with a sick person
- when you have been out in a public place
- after you use the toilet
- after you cough or sneeze
- before you eat or prepare food

Other things to do:

- Stay home when you are sick.
- Wash all items that others may touch, such as light switches, doorknobs, and telephones.
- If you get the flu, drink plenty of liquids, such as water, juices, and clear soups.

Sneeze into a tissue or into your sleeve. Throw away the tissue and wash your hands.

Use soap and count to twenty while you wash.

Stay home if you have a fever and feel sick.

27

Wonderful people!

Disasters are very hard on people. Many people lose their possessions. Some lose family members and friends. In every disaster, however, there are people who help others get through these terrible times. Before disasters occur, organizations such as the Red Cross prepare to respond to people in need. Other community helpers are also on the scene to rescue people and to treat the injured or sick. Firefighters put out fires and deal with dangerous chemicals. Rescue workers find people who are stranded and cannot get out. Healthcare volunteers, such as doctors, nurses, and paramedics, treat injured people.

Animals everywhere

There may be many animals, such as dogs or cats, wandering around your community after a disaster. Do not touch these animals. Some of them may be sick. Others may be shocked by what has happened. Shocked animals can behave in strange ways—they may bite or try to hurt you. If you see an animal, tell an adult to report it to volunteers in your community who are gathering the animals, treating their injuries, and finding people to care for them.

These volunteers are checking for injuries on a dog.

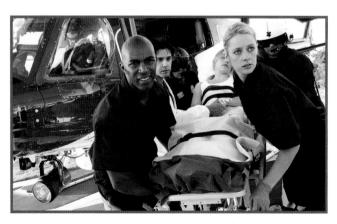

These rescue workers are bringing an injured girl to a hospital. She was flown to the hospital by a helicopter.

These kind Red Cross volunteers cheer up an elderly woman at a hurricane shelter.

Disastrous feelings

After a disaster, communities can look like war zones. It may not be safe to play outdoors for many months. Buildings may be unstable, and power lines may be spread across the ground. It is best not to touch anything! People who live through disasters can also feel damaged. They may feel angry, sad, or afraid. Feelings of fear can last long after the danger has passed.

Normal feelings

You may feel afraid that the disaster will happen again or that you will become separated from your family. These feelings can affect your appetite and sleep or those of your family members. All these feelings are normal but, eventually, you must face your fears and overcome them. A good way to overcome feelings of fear and sadness is by talking about your feelings and understanding that it is normal to feel the way you feel.

Sad feelings are normal after a disaster.

Express yourself!

You can express how you feel in other ways, too. You can draw pictures that show your feelings and fears. You and your friends can also write plays, play musical instruments, and act out what you have experienced. These activities will allow you to get out your feelings in a creative and fun way. It is very important to feel happy again!

Draw a picture about how you feel.

Playing music will make you feel better.

Going back to school makes kids feel that their lives are normal again.

Have fun with your friends!

29

More ways to prepare

What are some other things you can do to prepare for disasters? Make a list of other ways to prepare! Then suggest a family meeting and discuss your list with your family. Here are some ways you can get started.

Go camping!

Camping is a great way to explore nature and spend time with your family. It is also a great way to prepare for disasters! When disasters happen, people may have to sleep in tents, cook on portable stoves, bathe using only a bucket of water, and live without electricity. You can learn how to do all these things on a camping trip. You will feel a lot less stressed after a disaster if you have already done some of these things.

When you go camping, you can learn how to use a compass and read a map to find your way.

You can sleep in a tent and cook your food over a fire or on a portable stove. You can learn to "rough it."

Class time

Another way to prepare for disasters is by taking some classes that are offered in your community. Encourage your family to join you. You can learn important skills such as swimming, life-saving, and first aid. During emergencies, these skills could save your life, as well as the lives of others.

More things to do

- Learn the local emergency signals and sirens.
- Before a disaster happens, find out which agencies in your community would help you.
- Take a field trip to a police station or fire station.
- Ask your teacher to invite a Red Cross volunteer to speak at your school about disasters.

Keep learning!

You can never know too much about how to prepare for disasters. Learning more is the first step. Do research on the Internet with your parents or teacher to find out about disasters that can happen in your area. If you are going on vacation, research the place where you are going. What kinds of disasters happen in that area? When do they usually occur? Make sure you listen to weather reports every day—both when you are on vacation and when you are at home.

Red Cross volunteers can help you get prepared.

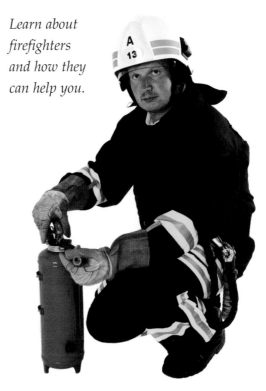

Learn about firefighters and how they can help you.

Find out more about disasters that could happen in your area. The Internet and library are great places to learn.

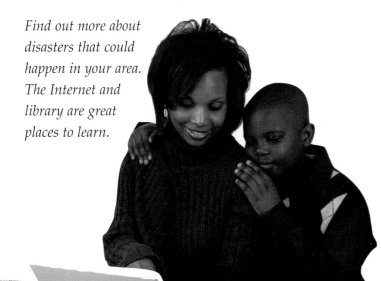

Be grateful that you and your family are alive!

Glossary

Note: Some boldfaced words are defined where they appear in the book.

aftershock A small earthquake that happens after a big earthquake

blackout A sudden loss of electricity

dam A wall built to hold back water

debris Scattered pieces of broken or damaged objects

disaster-supply kit A collection of items needed during and after a disaster

evacuate To leave or be forced to leave an area

eye The calm center of a hurricane

flash flood A flood that happens very quickly

human-made disaster A disaster that is caused by the actions of people

levee A hill built along a river to keep the river from overflowing

natural disaster A diaster that is caused by events in nature

plate Large rocks that are part of the Earth's crust on which the continents and oceans rest

storm surge Water pushed toward the shore by the winds of a storm

toiletries Items used in washing your body, such as soap, shampoo, and toothpaste

Tetra Pak A container that allows liquids to be stored at room temperature

Index

Web sites

American Red Cross: www.redcross.org

Canadian Red Cross: www.redcross.ca

Centers for Disease Control and Prevention: www.cdc.gov

National Weather Service: www.nws.noaa.gov

Environment Canada Weather office: www.weatheroffice.gc.ca/canada_e.html

Federal Emergency Management Agency (FEMA): www.fema.gov

Public Safety Canada: www.publicsafety.gc.ca

 Printed in the U.S.A.—CG